"What a delightful book! Not only is *Saints Alive* enjoyable and attractive, but it becomes a lively introduction to various saints: the old and the young, from different countries and social backgrounds, and many saints who would have remained unknown otherwise.

"The language of the saint-stories and the style and length of the charming prayers for each attest to Gayle Schreiber's awareness of what captures the attention of young children. The work pages are child-friendly, too, with large, simple designs that children love.

"While the book is aimed at teachers, parents of young children will be delighted with the help the book offers them to lead their tots to becoming "saints alive" now! I wish this book had been around when I was in the classroom."

Sr. Maxine Inkel, S.L.
Author, *100 Fun Ways to Livelier Lessons*

"This book is a treasure! What a wonderful resource to introduce our little ones to the Communion of Saints! The stories, prayers, and activity pages are lively and age-appropriate and present 'do-able' ways for young children to imitate the saints' love for God. This book introduces young children to models of our faith and helps form attitudes of holiness at a young age. I recommend it!"

Karen Leslie
Author, *Faith and Little Children*

"*Saints Alive* is very informative. The information presented on the individual saints is brief but very enlightening. Kindergarten students will become attentive when the stories are read. The activities that follow will be 'fun' for the students and remain as a reminder of the saint. Without hesitation. I recommend this book for any kindergarten teacher. It will prove a wonderful resource for any religion program."

Kathy Hrutkay
Principal, Holy Family School
Parma, OH

"Lucky are the children who will encounter this book in kindergarten. It is never too early to acquaint them with our saintly forebears, and it is never too early for our tots to follow in their saintly footsteps."

William Griffin
Author, *Jesus for Children:*
Read Aloud Gospel Stories

Saints Alive

Stories and Activities for Young Children

Gayle Schreiber

TWENTY-THIRD PUBLICATIONS
Mystic, Connecticut 06355

Twenty-Third Publications
185 Willow Street
P.O. Box 180
Mystic, CT 06355
(860) 536-2611
800-321-0411

ISBN 0-89622-675-1
Library of Congress Catalog Card Number 95-61491
Printed in the U.S.A.

Dedication

To my sister Sue Wistinghausen
who was the first to encourage me to write for publication.

Contents

Saints Alive

Stories and Activities for Young Children

Introduction

I am a kindergarten teacher, and for the past year I have been sharing saint stories with the children in my class. Knowing that many of the details in the lives of the saints can be very frightening for young children, I tried to focus on a positive aspect of each saint's story. I wanted the children to know that saints are people who chose to follow Jesus, and who tried to be good, kind, and generous. Many of them were ordinary people who made mistakes just like we do today. Yet they had tremendous love for Jesus.

I discovered that the children really enjoyed hearing these stories. As soon as they walked into the room they would ask if we were going to have a saint story. As part of the storytelling, I began devising activity pages that the children could color and take home to share with their families. These included a simple activity that could be done at home and a brief prayer. I had many favorable comments from parents. They liked the simple activities, and several said that they enjoyed learning about the saints with their children.

And so I share these stories, activities, and prayers with you, hoping that you will be inspired to use them with the little ones you teach. There are three stories for each month of the school year and one each for the months of June, July, and August.

Saint Gregory the Great

Feast Day: September 3

Let us pray.

Dear God,

thank you for

Saint Gregory.

Thank you for the

priests in our parish

and the teachers in

our school.

Help us to be good

listeners in church

and in school.

Amen.

Once there was a little boy whose name was Gregory. He was born in Rome. Gregory was a very quiet little boy who spent much time in prayer.

When he grew up, Gregory continued to spend quiet time in prayer. He was always very good to the poor. Gregory loved God very much and cared deeply about God's people.

Gregory became a priest and then he was chosen to be pope. He was a very good pope. He called himself "the servant of the servants of God." Gregory was very good at many things. He was especially good at preaching, teaching, and writing. He liked to preach and teach and write about God's goodness.

Gregory was named "Gregory the Great" because of all the good things he did in his lifetime. The name Gregory means watchman, and St. Gregory certainly did watch over God's people.

Gregory the Great is the patron saint of teachers.

Saint Gregory was a very good teacher. Color this apple for your teacher. Then say a prayer thanking God for everyone who is a teacher for you.

# ary, Mother of Jesus

Feast Day: September 8

Let us pray.

Dear God,

thank you

for giving us Mary,

the mother of Jesus.

Thank you for

our mothers, too.

Please help us to be

good children.

Amen.

Mary was born in a town called Nazareth, and she was a very good little girl. She did many nice things for people because she loved God and others very much.

Mary always showed concern for others. She knew that all her gifts and talents had come from God, and she talked to God often in prayer.

One day, God's messenger, the angel Gabriel, came to Mary and told her that she had been chosen by God to be the mother of the savior. Mary said "yes" to God's plan for her.

We honor Mary for being the mother of Jesus, but Mary is our mother, too. Her heart is very close to Jesus' heart. If we love others as Mary did, we are close to Jesus, too.

We give honor to Mary many times during the year and also on her birthday, September 8.

Mary is the mother of Jesus. Color and decorate this birthday cake for her. Sing "Happy Birthday" to Mary. Pray Mary's special prayer, the Hail Mary, with your family.

Saint Gabriel

Feast Day: September 29

Let us pray.

Dear God,

thank you for

special messengers,

such as the

angel Gabriel.

We want to be your

messengers, too,

telling everyone

about your love.

Thank you for

all those who tell us

about you. Amen.

The angel Gabriel was a special messenger of God who announced to Mary that she would be the mother of Jesus.

Much, much earlier, Gabriel had been sent to tell the prophet Daniel about the coming of Jesus, the long-awaited savior.

Closer to Mary's time, Gabriel was sent to a man named Zachary, who was married to Mary's cousin, Elizabeth. Gabriel told Zachary that Elizabeth would have a son whose name would be John. (When he grew up, John was called "the Baptist.")

All of the people that Gabriel gave messages to were willing to do God's will. When we want to do God's will, we should pray to the angel Gabriel for help.

Gabriel is the patron for postal workers who also deliver messages. Did you ever think of praying for those who deliver the mail? What a good idea!

6

The angel Gabriel was a special messenger of God. Color and decorate this envelope. Then draw a picture or write a note and send it to someone who is sad or lonely.

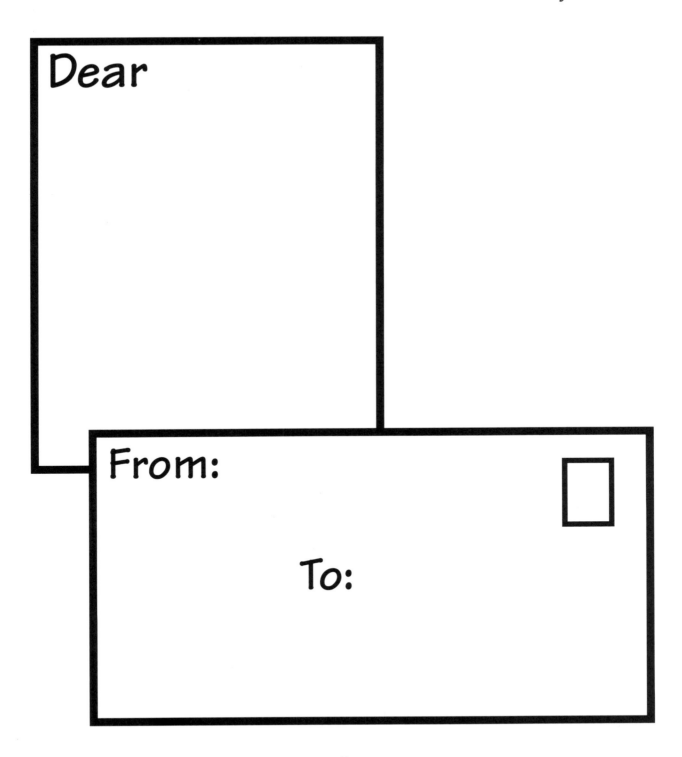

Dear

From:

To:

# Saint Thérèse

Feast Day: October 1

Let us pray.

Thank you, God,

for Saint Thérèse.

Help us to do all that

we can for Jesus,

as she did.

Help us to do many

small acts of love to

show our love for you.

Amen.

Once there was a little girl named Thérèse. She was born in France, and she had four sisters. Thérèse was a very religious child. She loved to go to church so much that she called Sundays "holidays."

Thérèse would often make little sacrifices for Jesus. She would try not to complain or not to use angry words. Every little act she did was for Jesus, even something as simple as picking up a pin.

Thérèse loved flowers. She noticed that although some flowers are more beautiful than others, God takes care of them all. She believed that God loves and cares for all people as well. Thérèse called herself the "little flower" of Jesus.

Thérèse and her four sisters all became nuns when they grew up. As a nun, Thérèse did simple jobs, like washing dishes, sewing, and cooking. She wanted to be close to God by doing simple little things very well, and that's what she always did.

Thérèse is the patron saint of missionaries because she always prayed for missionaries when she was a nun.

Saint Thérèse called herself the "little flower" of Jesus. Color this rose in your favorite color. If you can, plant a flower and give Jesus a "little kiss."

# Saint Francis

Feast Day: October 4

Let us pray.

Dear God, thank you

for Saint Francis.

Help us to love and

care for all of your

creatures as he did.

Thank you for

the sun and moon,

for birds and animals,

and for all of creation.

Amen.

Once there was a boy named Francis. His father was a wealthy cloth merchant in Assisi, Italy, and Francis had a very happy childhood. He had a life of fun as a teenager, too, by playing, singing, and going to parties.

When Francis was twenty years old, he fought in a war. He became ill during that time, however, and he had lots of time to think and pray. When Francis returned home, he decided that he wanted to change his ways and live only for Jesus.

Francis gave up all his beautiful clothes and his beautiful home. He lived a simple life, depending on God to provide for all his needs. Francis shared everything he had with the poor, and he spent much of his time teaching people about God.

Francis had a great respect for all of God's creatures. He loved nature, and he called animals, trees, the sun, and the moon his brothers and sisters. He is the patron saint of all those who study nature and find ways to care for our earth.

Saint Francis loved all of nature. Draw a bird in this tree and then color the tree. Do something special to show your love for nature today.

# Saint Luke

Feast Day: October 18

Let us pray.

Thank you,

loving God,

for Saint Luke.

Thank you, too,

for our doctors

who care for us

and for painters

who give us joy.

Help us to give joy

to others. Amen.

Once there was a man named Luke. He was a very good man who worked as a doctor.

One day he met a man named Paul. Paul told Luke many stories about Jesus, how Jesus helped people everywhere he went and made many sick people well. Luke and Paul became very good friends.

Luke learned everything he could about Jesus. He later wrote one of the four gospels which are in the Bible. In his gospel Luke says that Jesus loves all people and he always forgives us when we do something wrong if we are sorry.

Luke also wrote another book in the Bible. It is called "Acts of the Apostles." This book tells about life in the early church after Jesus was raised from the dead and went back to heaven.

Luke liked to paint. He painted beautiful pictures of Mary, the mother of Jesus. He is the patron saint of painters.

Saint Luke liked to paint. Draw a beautiful picture on the cover of this Bible. Ask a grown-up to read to you from Luke's gospel at bedtime today.

Saint Albert

Feast Day: November 15

Let us pray.

Thank you, dear God,

for Saint Albert.

Help us to study very

hard in school

so that we can learn

many things—

as Albert did.

Thank you for the

chance to study

and for our teachers.

Amen.

Once there was a priest named Albert. He was born in Italy, but when he grew up, he lived in France. There he became a teacher at the University of Paris. Albert loved to teach but he also loved to learn. He liked science, math, geography, religion, and he especially liked reading the Bible. He enjoyed sharing all that he learned with his students.

One creature that Albert enjoyed studying was the spider. Albert thought spiders were very interesting, and he thanked God for creating them.

Later Albert became a bishop. He would walk from town to town telling people about God and about God's creation. He was known as the "Bishop with the Boot" because he wore sturdy boots whenever he walked.

Saint Albert loved God's world. We can be like Albert by taking care of God's world. We can plant trees, put out bird feeders, and pick up litter. We can be like Albert when we study hard in school.

Albert is the patron saint of students.

Saint Albert loved to study. One creature he studied was the spider. Color this spider any color you want. Remember to study hard when you are in school or religion class.

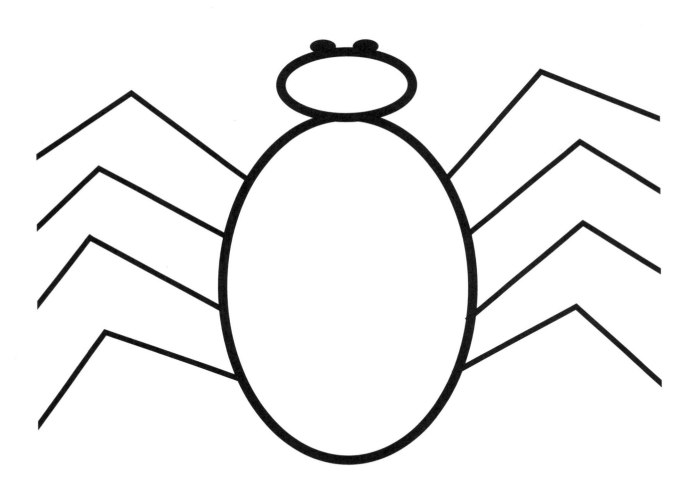

Saint Cecilia

Feast Day: November 22

Let us pray.

Thank you,

dear God,

for Saint Cecilia.

Thank you for

music and song,

and fun and dancing.

May we always sing

joyfully to you.

Amen.

Once there was a little girl named Cecilia. She was a very happy child who loved to sing and dance and play. She also liked to pray because she believed that Jesus loved her and watched over her always.

As she grew older, Cecilia wanted to give her life to Christ as a nun. But her parents wanted her to get married, and so she did.

After her marriage, Cecilia often talked to her husband and his brother about God. Soon they, too, became Christians. They both did all they could to help the poor, the sick, and anyone in need.

Cecilia was always kind to everyone. She loved all people, the rich and the poor. She loved music and she would often "sing to God in her heart." Her favorite musical instruments were the organ, the harp, and the viola.

Cecilia is the patron saint of musicians.

Saint Cecilia loved music. Color this musical note any color you want. Then sing your favorite song to God "in your heart."

Saint Andrew

Feast Day: November 30

Let us pray.

Thank you,

loving God,

for Saint Andrew.

We want to be

followers of Jesus—

as Andrew was.

Help us to share our

love for Jesus

with others. Amen.

Once there was a little boy named Andrew. His father was a fisherman, and Andrew grew up to be a fisherman, too. One day Andrew met Jesus, and Jesus told him about God and how important God's Word is. After that, Andrew gave up his work as a fisherman to follow Jesus. (A person who is a follower of Jesus is called an apostle or disciple.)

Andrew loved to be with Jesus. Once Jesus was talking to a large crowd of people, 5,000 of them. They were hungry and did not have food. Andrew told Jesus about a boy who had a few loaves of bread and some fish. The boy was willing to share his food, but it wasn't very much. Yet Jesus told Andrew and the others to start giving out the bread and fish. Guess what? There was enough to feed everyone—with lots left over.

After Jesus' resurrection from the dead, Andrew became a missionary (someone who teaches others about God). He talked to people about God in Greece, Turkey, and Russia. He was a very good man, and people always trusted him.

Andrew is the patron saint of fishermen.

Color the fish in this bowl. Then draw and color another fish of your own to keep this one company. Be a follower of Jesus today—like Andrew was—and tell others about Jesus.

# Saint Nicholas

Feast Day: December 6

Let us pray.

Dear God, thank you

for Saint Nicholas.

Let us always give

the gift of kindness

to others, as he did.

Thank you for

the gifts of love

we receive

from our families

and friends. Amen.

Once there was a boy named Nicholas who was born far away in Asia Minor. Nicholas was always good and kind. He liked to help people who were in need. When his parents died, Nicholas shared his money with the poor. When he grew up he became a monk, and later he became a bishop. He continued to show his love for God by loving and helping people.

For example, it is said that once there were three girls who were too poor to get married. Their father had no money to buy them the clothes and household goods they needed. One night Nicholas threw a bag of gold into each of their rooms. He didn't want them to know who had given them the money, but they knew it was Nicholas. He was always kind and generous to those in need.

After his death, people remembered the stories about Nicholas. People in the country of Holland called him Sinter Klaas. (In America this name was changed to Santa Claus.)

Nicholas is the patron saint of children.

Saint Nicholas was known for his kindness to everyone, especially to children. Trace and color the heart found "inside" this present. Let it remind you to show kindness to someone today.

# Saint Lucy

Feast Day: December 13

Let us pray.

We thank you

for Saint Lucy,

loving God.

Thank you for our

eyes that can see all

the beautiful things

you have made.

May we always

shine with your love.

Amen.

Once there was a little girl named Lucy. She was a kind and gentle girl who loved Jesus very much.

Lucy felt very sad when people did bad things to one another because she believed that all people shared God's love and should love one another as God's children. Although Lucy's family was wealthy, when she grew up she gave everything she owned to the poor.

Lucy liked to talk to God in prayer, and this made her faith very strong. She had beautiful, sparkling eyes and people could see God's love shining from them. In fact, the name Lucy means light.

Her feast day is celebrated during the season of Advent. In that season we await the coming of Jesus, the "light of the world." In Sweden, children celebrate Saint Lucy's feast day by wearing a crown of candles.

Because Lucy's eyes were so filled with light and love, she is the patron saint of those with eye diseases.

Saint Lucy is the patron for diseases of the eye. Color the eyes here the same color as your eyes. Use your eyes today to look at something God has created and then say a prayer of thanks.

# aint Stephen

Feast Day: December 26

Let us pray.

Thank you,

dear God,

for Saint Stephen.

Help us to be as

loving and forgiving

as he was. Thank you

for always forgiving

us when we make

mistakes. Amen.

Once there was a boy named Stephen. He loved Jesus very much, and when he grew up he became a deacon. (A deacon is a special person in the church who helps others.) Stephen helped the poor. He also helped children whose parents had died. He was a very good man.

Stephen was not afraid to tell others about Jesus and to stand up for what he believed in. He knew all about forgiveness, too. He knew that Jesus always forgives us if we do something wrong.

Stephen wanted to be like Jesus, so he would always forgive others. If someone said something mean to him, he would forgive them. If someone hit him or hurt him, he would forgive them. Once an angry group of men threw stones at Stephen. He forgave them and asked God to forgive them, too.

Stephen is the patron saint of deacons.

The name Stephen means "crown." Decorate this crown any way you like. Try to be like Stephen today by helping others and forgiving those who have hurt you.

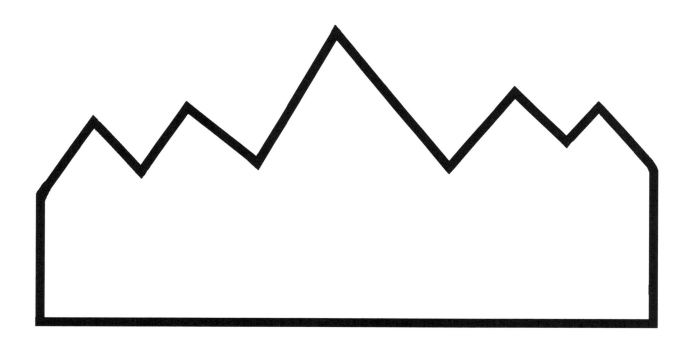

aint Elizabeth Ann Seton

Feast Day: January 4

Let us pray.

Thank you for Saint

Elizabeth, dear God.

Thank you for giving

us schools to go to

so we can learn

and grow. Help us to

listen to our parents

and teachers with

respect. Amen.

Once there was a little girl who was born in New York City. Her name was Elizabeth, but her friends called her Betsy. She was always a kind little girl who loved to help people.

Elizabeth got married when she grew up, and she had five children. She was a wonderful wife and mother. She also continued to care for the needs of others, especially the poor and the sick.

Elizabeth's husband died at a young age, and after his death, Elizabeth put her trust in God to guide her. She became a Catholic and moved with her children to Baltimore, Maryland.

Elizabeth opened the first Catholic school for girls in Baltimore. She had many followers to help her and soon they were known as the Sisters of Charity. After her death, Elizabeth became the first person born in the United States to be named a saint.

Elizabeth Ann Seton is the patron saint of Catholic schools.

Saint Elizabeth Ann Seton started a Catholic school for girls. Color this schoolhouse and remember to be a good listener and learn all that you can in school.

# Saint Agnes

Feast Day: January 21

Let us pray.

Dear God, thank you for Saint Agnes.

Help us to be as kind and gentle to others as she was, and let us be your "little lambs" who give joy and happiness to everyone around us. Amen.

Once there was a young girl in Rome named Agnes. Agnes loved simple things. Her favorite dress was plain white. People who saw her wearing this dress on the way to school said that she looked as pretty as a flower. They called her "a charming blossom."

Agnes was always gentle and sweet like a little lamb. She always thought of others. She was warm hearted with cheeks as pink as roses and eyes as blue as the sky. Agnes enjoyed being kind to others.

When she was only 13, Agnes was killed because she refused to give up her Christian faith. (People who die for their faith are called martyrs.)

Because of her gentle and pure ways, Agnes is still known today as "the little lamb of Jesus."

Agnes is the patron saint of young girls.

Saint Agnes was called the "little lamb of Jesus." Color this lamb, and then smile and show kindness to everyone you meet today.

29

Saint John Bosco

Feast Day: January 31

Let us pray.

Thank you, loving God, for Saint John Bosco. Please help all the children in our world who are poor and who have no schools to go to. Help us to value our education. Amen.

Once there was a boy named John who grew up in a very poor neighborhood. There children would often fight with one another in the streets.

One night John had a dream that God wanted him to take care of boys who were in trouble. John decided to do what God asked of him. When he grew up, he became a priest and he cared for orphan boys.

John would plan very special Sundays for these boys. They would travel to the countryside where John would celebrate Mass, and then they would share breakfast and games. The games would be followed by a picnic lunch and a lesson, and they would close the day with prayer.

The boys loved John because he made them feel important. Soon there were so many homeless boys that John needed more help. Other men joined him in this work, and today John's followers are still teaching poor children. Once John started a "cheerful club" for his boys. Members of this club tried to speak kindly to everyone.

John Bosco is the patron saint of young people.

Saint John Bosco was very kind to homeless boys. He taught them about Jesus and he also taught them to be shoemakers. Color this shoe. Then, make believe you are in John Bosco's "Cheerful Club" today and say only kind words to everyone.

# aint Bridget

Feast Day: February 1

Let us pray.

Dear God, thank you for Saint Bridget.

Help us to share what we have with others, as she did.

Thank you for giving us places to go to for prayer and learning about you. Amen.

Once there was a little girl named Bridget who lived in Ireland. She was a happy child who loved animals and music. She was full of joy and loved to share what she had with others.

Once Bridget saw a man who was very ill. The man did not have any money. Bridget gave him her father's expensive sword. Another time a woman gave her a basket of apples. Bridget gave them all away to people who were hungry.

Bridget worked in a dairy. She loved to care for the cows. She often gave their milk away to people in need. It is said that once she gave away a bucket of milk that her mother needed. Bridget was afraid that her mother would be mad so she prayed very hard, and God refilled the bucket with milk.

When Bridget grew up she became a nun. She and her followers lived in little huts made of clay that they made themselves. Bridget started a convent in the city of Kildare. It was a place where people could go to learn about God and to pray.

Bridget is the patron saint of dairy workers.

Saint Bridget loved to share. Color this picture. Then share a glass of milk and cookies or another snack with a family member today.

# Saint Blase

Feast Day: February 3

Let us pray.

Thank you

for Saint Blase,

loving God.

May we always be

grateful for good

health and may our

throats always sing out

your praise. Amen.

Once there was a doctor named Blase. He was a good doctor, and he cared very much about his patients. He worked hard to make them well.

Although Blase enjoyed his work, he knew that people needed God in their lives to be *really* well. He wanted to teach people about God's love, and so he became a priest. Later he became a bishop. Blase loved to pray and to preach to his people. He tried to help everyone he knew.

One day a woman brought her little boy who was choking on a fish bone to Blase. Blase saved the boy. After this he was known as someone who could heal diseases of the throat.

In our parishes today we still have the "blessing of throats" on the feast of Saint Blase. This blessing is given using two unlit candles crossed and tied with a ribbon.

Blase is the patron saint of those with diseases of the throat.

Saint Blase once saved a boy who was choking on a fish bone. Color the ribbon on these candles, and then color the candles. Say a prayer to Saint Blase to protect your throat from disease.

aint Valentine

Feast Day: February 14

Let us pray.

Dear God, thank you

for Saint Valentine.

Help us to show love

and kindness

to everyone we meet.

Thank you for all the

people who love us.

Amen.

Once there was a very holy priest named Valentine. Valentine lived in Rome and he wanted to serve God by living the gospels and following Jesus. These were his favorite words from Jesus: "Love one another as I have loved you." Valentine believed that God loves everyone very much, and he tried to show God's love in his dealings with others.

At that time in Rome, some people did not know Jesus. They did not like Valentine because he followed Jesus. These people put him in prison because he practiced his faith.

While in prison, Valentine wrote little messages to all of his friends to tell them that he loved them. In honor of him we send little messages or cards to people we love on Valentine's Day.

Valentine is the patron saint of engaged couples.

Saint Valentine loved all people—as Jesus does. Color this heart and ask Valentine to help you love Jesus. Hug your mom and dad today and tell them that you love them.

# aint Matilda

Feast Day: March 14

Let us pray.

Dear God, thank you for Saint Matilda.

Please watch over all people who are sick and keep them in your loving care.

Please watch over our brothers and sisters and our parents. Help us to be a good family.

Amen.

Once there was a little girl named Matilda who lived with her grandmother. She was a very good little girl who loved Jesus very much.

When Matilda grew up, she married a very nice man. They had five children. Matilda and her husband loved their children and they were good parents. Matilda and her husband taught their children to know Jesus. They taught them how to pray.

One sad day Matilda's husband died. After his death, Matilda's children were unkind to her. They took away everything that belonged to her. Matilda went to live in a convent. She was very poor there, but she felt rich because Jesus loved her.

Some time later, Matilda's children said they were sorry about how they had treated her. They gave her back her things. She used all of her money to build hospitals and churches. She spent the rest of her life doing good deeds. She forgave her children and never stopped praying for them.

Matilda is the patron saint of parents of large families.

Saint Matilda prayed to Jesus often. Decorate the lace on these praying hands. Sometime today, fold your hands and say a prayer to Jesus.

Saint Patrick

Feast Day: March 17

Let us pray.

Thank you, loving

God, for Saint Patrick.

Thank you for the

clover that grows

in the fields and

reminds us of your

loving presence.

We pray this

in Jesus' name.

Amen.

Once there was a little boy named Patrick who lived in Great Britain. When he was sixteen years old he was captured by pirates and taken to Ireland.

Patrick worked as a slave, taking care of sheep in the mountains. He spent much of his time praying to God. He felt very close to God. And then one day, Patrick escaped from Ireland.

When he got back home, he made the decision to become a priest. Later he became a bishop and he went back to Ireland to teach the people about Jesus. He traveled from village to village talking about God. He used a green shamrock that grew in the countryside to teach the people that God is Father, Son, and Holy Spirit.

Patrick was a good man. He was even kind to his enemies. He wrote many prayers and he built the first Christian church in Ireland.

Patrick is the patron saint of Ireland.

Saint Patrick loved God very much. He was kind to everyone. We can be like Patrick when we are kind to others. Color this shamrock green, and then make the Sign of the Cross.

# Saint Joseph

Feast Day: March 19

Let us pray.

Thank you, dear God, for Saint Joseph.

Thank you for our fathers who love and care for us.

Please watch over and bless our fathers and help them to do their jobs well. Amen.

Once there was a very good and gentle man named Joseph. He was in love with a very special girl named Mary. The angel Gabriel came to Joseph in a dream and told him that Mary was to be the mother of Jesus. Joseph was to be the foster father of Jesus. Joseph always obeyed God. He immediately became a strong protector for Mary. When Jesus was born, Joseph was also a strong protector for him.

Joseph was a simple man, and he worked all day in his carpenter shop. He must have been a very holy man because God chose him to watch over Jesus. Joseph was a wonderful husband and father. He trusted God in everything.

Jesus must have loved his foster father very much, and he probably enjoyed working with him in the carpenter shop. Jesus always obeyed and helped his parents.

Joseph is the patron saint of fathers and carpenters.

Saint Joseph was a carpenter. You can be a carpenter right now by finishing this house. Then say a special prayer of thanks for your father and the work he does.

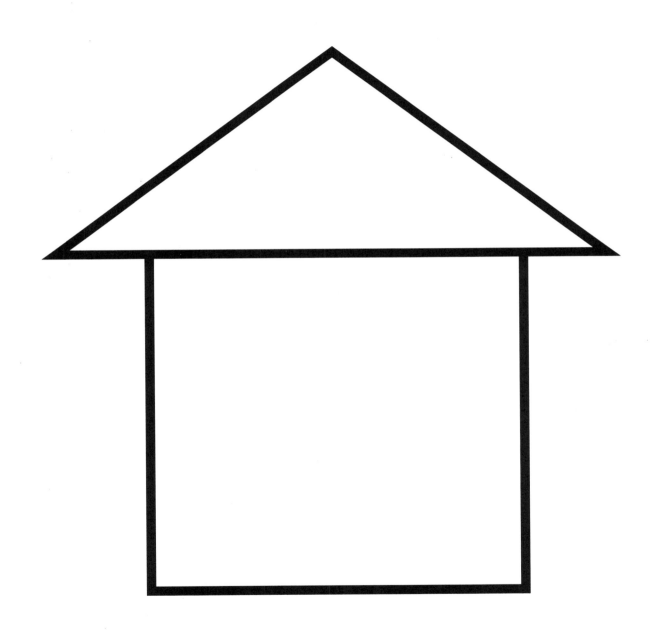

Saint Bernadette

Feast Day: April 16

Let us pray.

Dear God, thank you for Saint Bernadette. Help us to listen to your messages to us and to tell others about your great love. Thank you for giving us Mary, our mother. Amen.

Once there was a little girl named Bernadette who lived in Lourdes, France. Bernadette's family was very poor. One day Bernadette went out to find some firewood and Mary, the Mother of Jesus, appeared to her. Mary taught Bernadette how to make the sign of the cross and how to pray the rosary.

Mary asked Bernadette to pray for sinners (people who are very selfish). She also asked Bernadette to do penance for sinners (little deeds or prayers to make up for sin). Finally, Mary asked Bernadette to tell the bishop to build a shrine, a special place where people could come and pray to Mary. Bernadette did all that Mary asked of her.

When she grew up, Bernadette became a nun. She enjoyed working in the kitchen in the convent and praying to Mary and Jesus. The pope called Bernadette the "Lily of Mary."

Today people still go to Lourdes to pray at Mary's shrine. Many sick people have been cured there. Bernadette is the patron saint of those who do penance.

Saint Bernadette was known as the "Lily of Mary." Color this lily any color you want. Then say a prayer to Mary asking her to watch over you and your family.

# aint George

Feast Day: April 23

Let us pray.

Dear God, thank you for Saint George.

Help us to be as brave as he was and to always choose what is right. Thank you for our beautiful world, with its flowers and fields and trees.

Amen.

Once there was a very brave soldier named George. He told all good Christian people to be brave. He also told the people to pray often and to trust God.

It is said that one day a terrible dragon came to the town where George lived. The dragon poisoned the land with his fiery breath. He was so mean and wicked that he ate all the sheep in the town.

One day George decided to go out and kill that wicked dragon. The king was very happy and he wanted to give George a reward. George did not want a reward. Instead, he wanted the king to promise to build churches and to honor church leaders. He wanted the people to plant flowers and trees to make the land beautiful once again.

George loved the land God created. He loved people, too. And most of all, George loved God.

George is the patron saint of farmers.

Saint George is the patron saint of farmers. Draw flowers and trees in this picture that might be growing from the seeds in the ground. Plant some flowers in your own yard at home today.

# aint Catherine of Siena

Feast Day: April 29

Let us pray.

Thank you, loving God, for Saint Catherine. May we, too, feel the warmth of your love shining through us like the sun. May we praise your name and thank you every day for all the good things you give us. Amen.

Once there was a little girl named Catherine. She was the youngest of 23 children. Catherine wanted a room of her own so she could pray quietly. Her mother felt that she should help with housework more and pray less.

When Catherine was six years old, it is said that she saw Jesus standing above the church. She knew then that she wanted to be a nun. When she grew up, Catherine did become a nun, but she lived at home, and she spent all her time in her room praying. She only left her room to go to Mass.

One night Jesus spoke to her and told her that she could serve him best by serving others. So, Catherine began to leave her room to visit prisoners to tell them about Jesus. She brought food and clothing to the needy, and she continued to pray for all of God's people. Once Catherine even scolded the pope for not doing what God wanted. She was very brave.

Catherine once said that she saw God as the brightness of the sun. She could feel the fire of God's love in her soul. For this reason, Catherine is the patron saint of fire prevention.

Saint Catherine could feel the warmth of God's love. Color this sun. Then sit quietly and feel the warmth of God's love surround you.

# Saint Monica

Feast Day: May 4

Let us pray.

Dear God, thank you

for Saint Monica.

Help us to put

our faith in you

and to pray for others

as Monica did.

Bless our families

and help them

to grow in faith.

Amen.

Once there was a little girl named Monica who lived in a very loving home. Her mother was very kind and she taught Monica to know Jesus.

When Monica grew up she got married. Her husband was not always kind to her, but Monica was a peacemaker. Monica and her husband had three children. Monica set a very good example for her husband and children. She prayed often and she went to Mass daily.

Most of all, Monica did good deeds for others to show her love for God. Her good deeds included always being kind and gentle to everyone.

Monica asked God to make her husband a better person, and God did. She also asked God to help her son, Augustine, to become a Christian. And God answered that prayer, too.

Monica is the patron saint of mothers.

Saint Monica showed her love for Jesus by doing good deeds for others. Color one petal on this flower for each good deed that you have done today.

# Saint Bernard

Feast Day: May 28

Let us pray.

Thank you, loving

God, for Saint Bernard.

Just as he helped

others, so may we help

our parents today.

Thank you, too, for our

animals who give us

love and protection.

Amen.

Once there was a boy named Bernard who was born in Italy. When he grew up, he became a priest. Bernard built many churches and schools to teach people of God's love.

Later Bernard became a missionary in the Swiss Alps. Bernard taught the people there about Jesus. He also built two houses in the mountains to help travelers who were lost. These houses were named Great and Little Bernard.

Because Bernard spent much of his time rescuing lost people in the mountains, he trained special dogs to help him. Today these dogs are called "Saint Bernards."

Saint Bernard was a very good man. He helped people whenever he could. He never got tired of telling people about God's love for them.

Bernard is the patron saint of mountain climbers.

Saint Bernard's name means bold as a bear. Color this bear and remember how brave Bernard was when he helped lost travelers in the mountains. Be a good helper to your mom and dad today.

Saint Joan of Arc

Feast Day: May 30

Let us pray.

Dear God, thank you for Saint Joan of Arc. Help us to be as brave as she was and to always listen to your voice. May we offer your peace and love to everyone we meet today. Amen.

Once there was a little girl named Joan who was born in France. She had four brothers and sisters. Joan liked to sew and she learned to be a very good housekeeper. She also tended the sheep and rode on her horse. She was a very happy child who loved to pray.

Joan did special things to show her love for God. She was kind to the sick. She gave to the poor whenever she could. She went to Mass often.

One day, an angel appeared to Joan and told her that she would be a soldier. She would lead her country in war. Joan told the angel that she would do as God wanted. She rode into battle carrying a banner with the names Jesus and Mary on it.

Joan was very, very brave. She knew that God was always with her, and she wanted peace, not war.

Joan of Arc is the patron saint of soldiers.

Saint Joan of Arc loved Jesus and Mary. Trace the words Jesus and Mary on this banner and then color it. Say a prayer for peace today and pray for children who live in places of war.

Saint Peter

Feast Day: June 29

Let us pray.

Thank you, loving

God, for Saint Peter.

Thank you, too,

for our church leaders.

May we always listen

to your voice speaking

through them.

And thank you for

forgiving us when we

make mistakes. Amen.

Once there was a fisherman named Simon. One day he met Jesus, and Jesus asked him to come follow him. He wanted Simon to help him to tell people about God. Simon said yes, and he began to follow Jesus.

Jesus changed Simon's name to Peter because Peter means "rock." Jesus said that he would build his church on this rock. He meant that he wanted Peter to lead all those who would soon be called Christians.

Peter was a very kind, generous, and simple man. But he sometimes made mistakes—just like you and me. Peter even lied once. He told someone that he did not know Jesus. Peter did this because he was afraid of being arrested himself. Jesus knew that Peter was very sorry for what he had done, and he forgave him.

After Jesus died, Peter continued to tell people about God and to lead the other followers. Peter is the patron saint of those who follow Jesus.

Saint Peter was the rock of the church, but he sometimes made mistakes. Yet Jesus always forgave him. Color this rock and then ask Saint Peter to help you to follow Jesus.

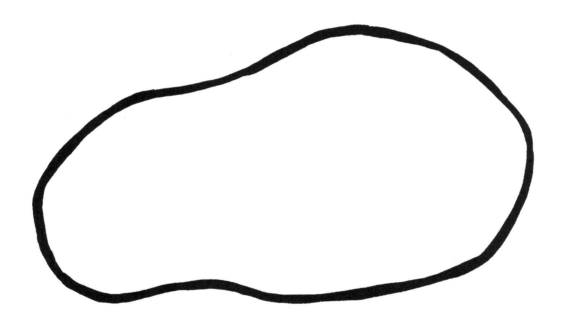

# Saint Martha

Feast Day: July 29

Let us pray.

Thank you, God,

for Saint Martha.

Help us to cheerfully

help with chores at

home, but also teach

us how to pray.

Thank you for our

parents who do so

much for us. Amen.

Once there was a girl named Martha. She lived with her sister, Mary, and her brother, Lazarus. When they grew up, Martha, Mary, and Lazarus were all very good friends of Jesus. They lived in a town named Bethany, which was near the city of Jerusalem.

Jesus would often visit their home, and Martha loved to cook for Jesus. She loved to serve Jesus, but sometimes she worked too hard. Jesus taught Martha that it is also important to spend quiet time listening to God.

Martha believed in Jesus and in everything that he taught her. When Lazarus died, Martha sent for Jesus. She knew that he would help them, and guess what? Jesus brought Lazarus back to life. Martha and her sister, Mary, were so happy to have their brother back.

After Jesus' death and resurrection, it is said that Martha traveled all over, telling people about Jesus.

Martha is the patron saint of cooks.

Saint Martha loved to cook for Jesus. Color this slice of bread the color of your favorite jelly. Make a peanut butter and jelly sandwich today and share it with someone you love.

aint Rose

Feast Day: August 23

Let us pray.

Dear God, thank you for Saint Rose.

Help us to be as kind and loving as she was.

Help us, too, to be helpful in every way to our parents and teachers. Thank you for the gift of flowers. Amen.

Once there was a little girl named Isabella. She was very beautiful. Her cheeks were so rosy that her mother began to call her Rose.

Rose worked in the garden and did needlework. She liked to sew flowers because she loved flowers. Rose also loved to pray. She built a little hut for herself in the backyard and she would often go there to pray.

When Rose grew up she became a nun. Her parents were very poor and they needed money. Rose sold her needlework and flowers to help them.

Rose loved all poor people. She set up a room in her parents' home to provide free care for old people who were sick. She was a very kind person.

Rose is the patron saint of florists.

Saint Rose loved flowers. Draw some flowers in this vase.
Then offer to water your mom's plants today.

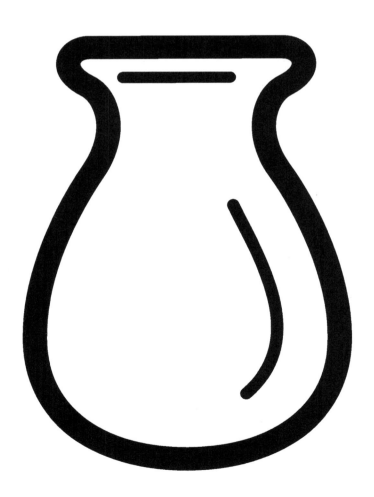

Of Related Interest ...

The Book of Saints
Michael Walsh
Here is a saint for each week of the year. Each saint's biography opens with an illuminated capital that depicts a scene or notable quality identified with that saint. Reader's encounter with these saints can serve to renew their own commitment to faith, prayer and loving service.
0-89622-628-X, 160 pp, $9.95 (order M-20)

Celebrating Holidays
20 Classroom Activities and Prayer Services
Stacy Schumacher and Jim Fanning
The authors of this book for religion teachers of the intermediate grades give a decidedly spiritual dimension to traditional secular holidays such as Columbus Day, President's Day, Labor Day, Earth Day, and April Fool's Day.
0-89622-611-5, 128 pp, $12.95 (order M-10)

Leading Students Into Scripture
Sr. Mary Kathleen Glavich
Presents a wide range of methods to help children understand the Bible.
0-89622-328-0, 112 pp, $9.95 (order W-18)

Learning by Doing
150 Activities to Enrich Religion Classes for Young Children
Carole MacClennan
A systematic yet simple "lesson wheel" approach where the lesson is seen as a wheel with a hub (topic) that is connected by spokes (sensory activities designed to engage the attention of young children) to the rim (completed ojetives)
0-89622-562-3, 128 pp, $14.95 (order C-07)

100 Fun Ways to Livelier Lessons
Maxine Inkel
Designed to enhance regular religion studies, this is a treasure chest of lively lessons based upon notable Catholic persons, events and seasons, as well as civic holidays and feasts observed by other faiths.
0-89622-654-9, 128 pp, $12.95 (order M-41)

Prayers, Activities, Celebrations (and more) for Catholic Families
Bridget Mary Meehan
Encourages families to come together for exercises and activities that reinforce their faith, strengthen family ties and solidify Catholic values.
0-89622-641-7, 72 pp, $7.95 (order M-38)

When Jesus Was Young
Carole MacClennan
Helps children in grades K-5 understand the life and times of Jesus through activities such as grinding wheat for bread or weaving a mat.
0-89622-485-6, 80 pp, $7.95 (order C-58)

Available at religious bookstores or from:

TWENTY-THIRD PUBLICATIONS
XXIII P.O. Box 180 • Mystic, CT 06355 • 1-800-321-0411